MW00892512

Music is my life and my life is music.

-Mozart

TrantBooks

MUSIC NOTATION GUIDE

STAFF
- The Staff (or Stave) is made up of five horizontal lines that are numbered from bottom to top
- The bottom line is the First Line and the top line is the Fifth Line
- Each line and space on the Staff represents a different musical pitch or tone
- Music is written on the lines and in the spaces of the Staff

GRAND STAFF
- When two staves are joined together it is called a Grand Staff or Great Stave

Treble Clef
- The top staff/stave is called the Treble Clef

Bass Clef
- The bottom staff/stave is called the Bass Clef

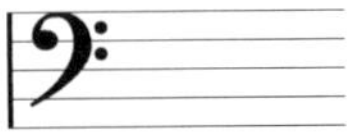

- In piano, the right hand plays the Treble Clef and the left hand plays the Bass Clef

BARS AND BAR LINES
- The vertical lines on the staff/stave are called Bar Lines
- The spaces in between the Bar Lines are called Bars
- Two vertical lines are called a Double Bar Line
- The Double Bar Line means the end of the piece or section of music

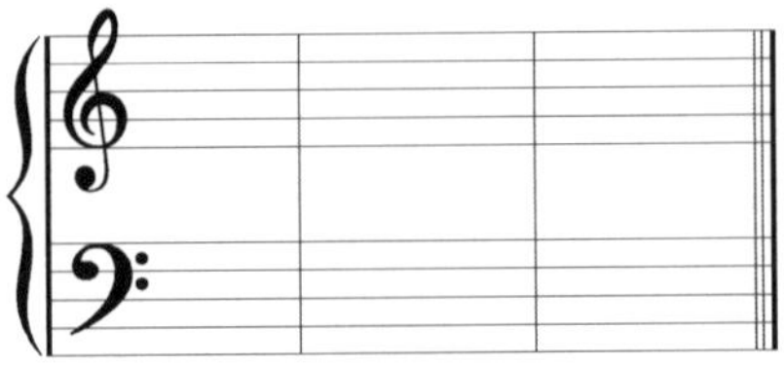

TIME SIGNATURES
- The top number shows the number of beats per Bar
- The bottom number shows the type of Note being counted

4 quarter notes per bar

6 eighth notes per bar

NOTES

- Notes (or keys) are placed on the lines and in the spaces of the Staff

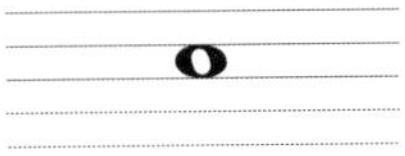

- There are seven letters used for music notes

A B C D E F G

Treble Clef Line Notes

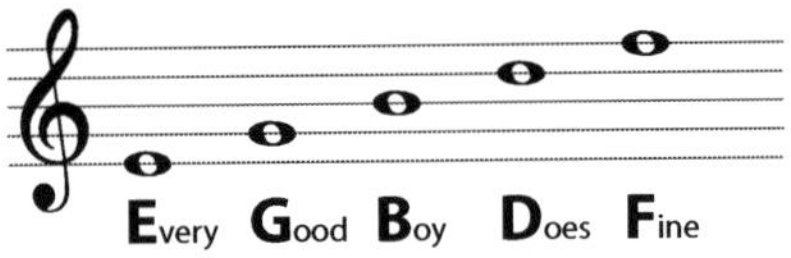

Every **G**ood **B**oy **D**oes **F**ine

Bass Clef Line Notes

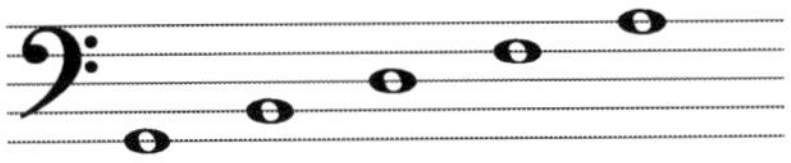

Great **B**ig **D**ogs **F**all **A**sleep

Treble Clef Space Notes

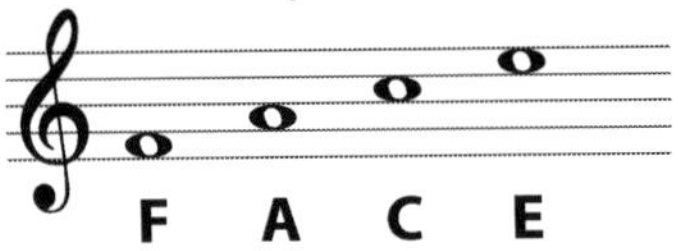

F A C E

Bass Clef Space Notes

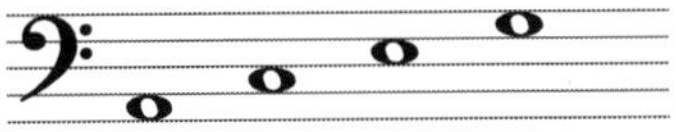

All **C**ows **E**at **G**rass

SYMBOL	NOTE (4/4 Time)
	Whole Note (Play for 4 beats)
	Half Note (Play for 2 beats)
	Quarter Note (Play for 1 beat)
	Eighth Note (Play for 1/2 a beat)
	Sixteenth Note (Play for 1/4 beat)

RESTS

- Silence in music is represented by Rest symbols

SYMBOL	REST (4/4 Time)
	Whole Rest (Rest for 4 beats)
	Half Rest (Rest for 2 beats)
	Quarter Rest (Rest for 1 beat)
	Eighth Rest (Rest for 1/2 a beat)
	Sixteenth Rest (Rest for 1/4 beat)

DID YOU KNOW
In American English "Staff" is more commonly used and in British English it's "Stave". In both cases the plural is "Staves".

20532146R00057

Made in the USA
Middletown, DE
10 December 2018